PRAISE FOR S.T. CARTLEDGE

"Stunning imagery and language use that plain blows the doors off the ordinary or conventional."

- CHRISTINE MORGAN, AUTHOR OF THE RAVEN'S TABLE

Beautiful and haunting poetry that manages to be both terse and full. Cartledge's ability really shines when he's chewing the scenery, creating fireworks with a few well-placed words. And in that gaping wound is where he injects the heart; the soul of each poem.

- DANGER SLATER, AUTHOR OF I WILL ROT WITHOUT YOU

PIXEL BOY IN POETRY WORLD

S.T. CARTLEDGE

CL4SH

Copyright © 2019 by S.T. Cartledge

Cover art by Lev Cantoral

levcantoral.com

CLASH Books

clashbooks.com

All rights reserved.

No part of this book may be reproduced in any form or by any electronic or mechanical means, including information storage and retrieval systems, without written permission from the author, except for the use of brief quotations in a book review.

For Dorothy Porter, whose verse novel, 'the Monkey's Mask' unfolded so many possibilities within myself.

year after year
on the monkey's face
a monkey's mask

- MATSUO BASHO

CONTENTS

BAPTISM	1
GLITCHED	2
FIRST BOSS	4
HOMESCREEN	6
POET IN A PIXEL WORLD	8
CIRCLES/SCREENS	10
NECK OF THE WORDS	11
PIXEL BOY IN POETRY WORLD	13
ABSOLUTE	15
POETRY GIRL	16
LOVE/HATE	18
THE LONGEST LINE	20
THE LOOP	22
THE POET'S DEN	24
MONOCHROME SKIES	26
A GAME OF POEMS	28
EXISTENTIAL PLAYER ONE	29
THE BOSS OF WORDS	31
SCREENSAVER	33
BAPTISM II	35
BEYOND THE BLACK PIXEL	38
REWRITTEN	40
BOOK TWO	42
FIRST SUMMER	43
PAINTED DRAGONS	45
AND THE CITY SLIPS AWAY	48
ATEMPORAL KOI POND	50
SHADOWPLAY	53
A TRAIL OF HAIKU	54
ENDLESS TSUNAMI	55
THE BRUSHSTROKE DRAGON	57

FESTIVAL OF THE PLACE THAT IS AND IS NOT HERE	59
BASHO MULTIPLIED ONE THOUSAND TIMES	61
NUJABES SYMPHONY IN THE SKY	63
DRAGON RAIN AND NIGHT-TIME WISDOM	65
DRAGON SONG	67
LOVE FOR THE THING THAT IS NOT REAL	69
POEM FLOWING RIVER REAL	71
PAINTING OF THAT BASHO FEELING	72
THE ILLUSTRATED WORLD OF HAIKU	74
FOUND DRAGON FRIEND	76
LOST DRAGON, BASHO FOUND	78
BASHO RAIN	80
Acknowledgments	81
About the Author	83
ALSO BY CLASH BOOKS	85
WE PUT THE LIT IN LITERARY	89

BAPTISM

He found himself baptised into a world of words.
He was saturated in a place which was unfamiliar,
drenched in the sickly sweet musk of love songs and
depression.
The sounds were not the synthesis of computers.
They were words desperately cried out from winged
beasts.
The words of winged poets: faceless and eyeless.
Only their mouths could speak.
Only screaming of their nightmares of this world.
They had convinced themselves their poetry fell on deaf
ears.
It did.
In this world, in the infinite history of the world
stretching in reverse, it did.

And then Pixel Boy was born.

He was baptised.

GLITCHED

This level is like no other one he has come across before.
The other side of the portal is a strange place.
It touches him beyond the pixels which make up his image.
It scratches like a tortured widow's pen, madly, across a page.

A hand moving in three dimensions.

She doesn't use ink.

There is no illumination on a screen.

This is the tactile plane of poetry.

It is the fuzzy memory of home –
the vectors forming the shapes of love and death.
The twin sweethearts of this mirror world.
Reflecting and amplifying.

In his head, the stray programming,
the lucid commands of something other, a glitch.
A level not meant for such sprites.
There is no direction for him, no instructions.

He is lost.

FIRST BOSS

The mother of love came down from the skies.
Her eyes were a million different versions
of the same shade of blue.

A crystal by any other light.

She is suspended by a series of strings, pulleys, and levers.
Her game mechanisms are invisible to the untrained eye.

She moves to the physics of her own words,
her love poetry and her body moving as one.

In this world she is swift and graceful,
yet her movements are wild and unpredictable
to Pixel Boy.

He dreams of the beautiful contrast of monochrome skies
against a side-scrolling landscape.

The safety of movement in two dimensions.

A pre-programmed boss fight,
the perfect timing of calculated movement and repetition.

The assault of a love poet,
the swoon of the lyrical song,
is a nightmare far worse than any digital boss
stealing all your lives.

HOMESCREEN

There is an ocean inside him,
crashing waves of white noise
and reminiscing of the homescreen.

A place of memory and comfort.
A place understood perfectly by all who exist within it.

He is synecdoche,
the part standing in for the whole,
the character for the game,
and all the other characters are ghosts
waiting for his return.

Right now, the homescreen exists without him.
It exists within him by proxy
like a shell taken from the beach
is a reminder of the beach.
The white noise waves call him back,
the bit-crushed ocean calls him back.

His objective in this level is to leave it.
His objective is to return to the homescreen.

His objective is to not die –
because who knows what will happen
when he is so far from home
his brain can no longer comprehend things
in terms of programs and commands,
objectives and video game mechanisms?

POET IN A PIXEL WORLD

There is a circle in the dirt,
a community of dirty demons,
wingless poets – faceless and eyeless.

The mouths of sealed parcels.

Behind their flat skin faces
– where their eye sockets are –
the glowing hum of pixel-vision,
poets without poems,
poets yet to earn their wings, their voices,
hypnotised by the video game screen.

A circle in the dirt,
around a screen sunk into the ground,
they brush the dirt away from it
and seize their controllers.

There is a sprite on the screen,
an internal monologue following him,

directing him, navigating him with prose.

The poets read every line
and study every object
for a sign that greater meaning exists
somewhere embedded deep within the game.

CIRCLES/SCREENS

The trauma poets are everywhere,
their deranged rants carry their words through the wind,
a vortex mixing them into a confused choir,
sweeping them around, carried
like the ash of a world long since burned to nothing.

All other levels are erased.

Throughout the world there are countless circles,
poets hypnotised by the screens in the ground,
hypnotised by the video games
which seemed to have risen through the dirt
to the surface
coming from another world entirely.

NECK OF THE WORDS

He found that the longer he remained in this world
the more it changed around him,
the more it changed him.

The poets evolved into an array of convoluted nightmares.
They existed so violently and beautifully,
so real, yet so drastically imagined,
an infinitely expanding series of simulacra.

He wanders into the neck of the words
where the young poets go to find themselves –
a garden populated exclusively by cherry blossom trees
and the crisp sound of plucked strings and piped wind.

An eyeless girl meets Pixel Boy beneath a round arch
and her fingers explore the smooth edges of his face.

She whispers gently that
every poet exists within their own world,
every poet must search for the right words

to translate the beauty of their world
to the countless others, the others blind,
so that we too can share their beauty.

She tells him that she knows no other words yet.

Pixel boy says that she is the first beautiful thing
he has seen in this world
and that all the other things
were too sinister to be admired.

PIXEL BOY IN POETRY WORLD

The girl grabs Pixel Boy and pulls him by his block hands
into the dynamic void of poetry world.
The world swirls a vast array of words and colours,
a clarity beyond anything which he had seen before.

He catches a glimpse of what might be home.
A flickering of light.
A saturation of 8-bit colour.

If there is a portal into the world,
surely there must be a portal out of it.

She tells him about the chrome soldiers,
who came from other places either forgotten to the world
or places which never existed in this reality at all.

What became of them is a mystery,
while the history of this world remains a hurricane
which never sleeps or settles.

Finding a single portal to a digital dimension
in such an unstable plane of reality
would be nearly impossible,
no matter how profusely she apologises.
No matter how much she explains to him
the nature of the world.

Only
strange things happen for unknown reasons.

ABSOLUTE

Like giant hammers falling onto the entire playing field,
he faces a level which may be impossible
for the first time.
His programming comes undone.

The only absolutes are love and death.
No restarts.
No return to menu.
No homescreen reunion.

And everywhere he looks,
love and death and poetry,
the world bleeding with its own mythos.

Poets in circles playing video games,
the video games of a generation of poets
whose art is abstract performance,
the study of simulation.

The game of poets gathers momentum by the day.

POETRY GIRL

As the world changes around them,
Pixel Boy and Poetry Girl fail to notice,
they too have changed.

The neck of the words where they met
has become mutilated by technology,
the cherry blossom trees
becoming high definition simulations,
the pipes and strings are crushed down,
digitally processed
as his world encroaches upon hers,
destroying something beautiful.

He wonders if this is happening
because he came here or
if he came here because of this.

She tries to cry real tears,
to mourn the death of the place

where poets go to find themselves.
She is lost, and only wet pixels drip
from the wells of her eyeless face,
the boarded-up windows to her poet's soul.

LOVE/HATE

Gone is the spirit of the winged poets.
The mother of love is ghostly
as the strings which guide her are ghosts.

Gone is the cryptic nature of words combined,
lost to the other dimension –
that of vectors, sprites, and
the linear progression towards a simple goal.

That which is not meant to be deconstructed or decoded.

It is in the programmed mind
of Poetry Girl
to take the world as she sees it,
(as she loathes it in its geometric form)
and translate its beauty as only her poetry can.

What words catch in her throat and break apart:
is this a poem of love for a new world crystallised

from a reality beyond her comprehension,
or a poem of the death of a world rapidly slipping
from her consciousness?

THE LONGEST LINE

One beginning and one end,
this is the world he came from,
the world he lost.

What became a video game pathogen
infecting a new world.
A disease infecting the mind
of himself
and/or
everyone around him.

A single line?
No.

While the endless possibilities unfolded
of multiple characters
executing myriad destinies
at the same time,
the sequences began to loop

and repeat
and pass over again,
like a level whose goal remained just out of reach.

THE LOOP

The screens have taken over.
The games are worlds of words
designed by unseen poets, trapping others
in their bodies,
in their minds a weightless euphoria,
a liberation from the poet's law.

Who these poets are,
or why they have orchestrated such a design
is beyond the understanding
of the others yet to be drawn into the loop.

He is amongst them, a fuzzy dream
witnessing those remaining creatures
calling themselves: chaos poets, or
nightmare poets.

What loops await them,
what limbo...
a future in screens designed

to keep the mind stimulated enough
to question reality but not enough
to challenge it.

He sees this future for Poetry Girl,
he sees this future for the chaos poets
and the nightmare poets.

The screens, the games,
the image and reflection
have been removed from reality.

What monsters would do this?

What poison would rot the ones you love to ruin?

What remains
are the echoes of love and death,
poetry and dust.

THE POET'S DEN

In the poet's den,
the last remaining poets
sit and wonder what it's like
to play the video game.

The pixel-rain is falling down,
oh the pixel-rain, it pours,
white noise on a tin roof,
and the chaos poets,
the nightmare poets
drown out the white noise
with their crooning lovesongs
and
deathsongs
oh the loss,
the pain
of waking
up,
the endurance of the people
versus

the endurance of the rain,
the game,
each pixel falling is a poem
gone,
rinsed away forever in the
computer.

The system restarts
and the poets continue to gather.

MONOCHROME SKIES

Stepping out
to a scene of moving platforms and projectiles,
floating items,
a wave of calm washes over him.

This is not his home,
nor the home of poets guided
by his protection.

This is a strange and dangerous
hybrid plane of worlds bisected
and madly contorted,
neither homescreen nor poet's page.

It is the uncanny liminal space
between the two, inseparable,
yet completely unfamiliar.

A trapdoor of sorts.

The monochrome skies have
hanging in their space, the words
which guide the world of poets
through their nightmare simulation
of a game-but-not-a-game, playing reality,
the words plastered on a floating plaque:

I WAS BORN UNDER MONOCHROME SKIES
TWILIGHT IS MY HEART AND SOUL
I AM THE PIXEL POET

A GAME OF POEMS

As the landscape rolls on,
the plaques hang in open air
and recite stanzas from the Pixel Poet.

Devices for the game.

The aimless challenge to decrypt
the words, the meaning, to figure out
what this world once was
and what it has since become.

Figure out
who is the Pixel Poet,
figure out
what the point is
to this game of poems.

EXISTENTIAL PLAYER ONE

The act of losing yourself.
The act of everything around you sinking into darkness.
A spotlight.

This place which is no longer place,
no longer a world of poets, the lyrical world of poetry
dripping into the existential plane of this.

All game, no control.
No rules or order, no direction.
Only the birth of something new, something different.
The birth of oxygen to a child's lungs,
the birth of blood to heart.

In the distant fog of mind patterns,
synapses forming thought,
to find the Pixel Poet beyond the veil
of immediate realities,
to destroy the machine and return
the world to a liberated zone.

Waves crashing in our minds.
The song of love and death, the beautiful nature of words
forming shapes, words thrown like stones
skipping on a flat lake.

What words combine to reveal a game
which is more than the sum of its parts,
words swirl and combine to reveal the fact that we exist
as everything around us exists.

Play on.

THE BOSS OF WORDS

In the blackened playing field
the game grows quiet,
an intense concentration floods
through the atmosphere.

Up ahead is the mouth of some
visceral madness,
the jaws of a decapitated poet,
a monster, a forest of teeth, broken angles
reaching from the ground, from the sky,
a warm cave, a mouth filled with blood
and a chaos storm of words.

The pink flesh walls are lit up by firelight
and tickled with gigantic shadows,
the wings of other poets hammered
into the gummy walls with metal stakes
and at the throat of the giant beast-corpse,
a dangling plaque reads:

I AM HERE

SCREENSAVER

There is so much static in the air
it could bring distant sleeping dragons to this world,
it could cross dimensions and reduce
everything to blank screens.

Instead, those poets which remain
sink into the mass of blood and gums,
all those left resisting the controller
become part of the soup of the world
now simulating other-worldly dangers.

Pixel Boy disappears into the hollow of the throat,
a passage disappearing, an adventurer swallowed whole.
Poetry Girl is a few steps behind,
evolving to the playing field,
jumping on the bones of other poets
to escape the sinking fate of the gumswamp.

Down a long hall,
his calling, the fated path which he must take,

he finds no boss of words nor sacred artefact,
not even a checkpoint or another plaque.

The infinite tree of all possibilities,
branching out and occupying spaces
beyond the plane of this reality,
it twists into a socket shaped exactly like
a Pixel Boy.

A world machine with arms outstretched,
receiving him.

The poetry of the world has died,
the love has died, swallowed by the machine
which has reached through portals into other worlds,
reached with teleporting limbs and found
the one thing which would reduce
the words of poets to ash.

The game, the simulation
where you project your consciousness
into another being and accept it as truth.
This reality which plays out then dies.
This reality which is born from nothing
and replays and transforms endlessly,
sessions on an unreal world.

Pixel Boy enters the socket,
he becomes part of the system
and Poetry Girl can only watch.

He feels the world around him dissolving,
he feels the homescreen calling his name.

BAPTISM II

Where has he gone, oh
where has he gone?

Did he know this portal would be his last?

Did he know he would be leaving
poor, cold, blind Poetry Girl behind?
Such sweet cubic tears fall
down the grace of her cheeks
to her little checker shoes.

This is not the homescreen.
This is something else.

A piano on a beach in a storm,
and the person playing does not know
how to play so he just
makes
it
up.

He has made mistakes for the last time,
not knowing how to begin again,
not knowing if he will be reborn,
not knowing if he will be again baptised
in the beauty of a foreign place.

Poetry world is a fever dream,
something so terrifyingly beautiful.
A world described in full vision
as only he can see it.

A lonely girl, lost for words,
abandoned.

A sun witnessed for the first time
etched its silhouette over the mountain ranges,
giving birth to new days.

He is swallowed whole by simulations
of things which happened to him,
things which he did over and over again,
things which happened
and transformed him.

His programming, his video game mechanisms
lost from his mind
as a new language has reprogrammed him
and baptised him in an ocean of words.

The past monstrosities of his billion lives
washed away,
the memory of poetry world

washed away,
leaving a gap shaped like people and places.

A feeling of something once loved,
forgotten.

BEYOND THE BLACK PIXEL

Where is this place?

This plane of reality neither tactile nor real.

A simulation.

Always a simulation.
The programming of minds split
into infinite simulations growing and transforming
and becoming ways to filter and
destroy the minds of unknown subjects.

He was here
and he knew who she was
and then he slipped into an imagined world
so far he slipped and he believed
that what he saw and felt and did
were real things,
he saw it as a game,

himself a program within it,
executing commands and functions,
possessed by screens and computers
and consumed by a logical reality
much simpler than his own.

REWRITTEN

He lost his way with words,
and she thought that if she played along with his charade
she could bring him back
and he could make sense of this world again.

He is broken, sure.
Maybe a little scarred.
But he is here in the real world,
seeing it for what it is
and for who he is

genuinely

for the first time.

He looks at her as he would a stranger,
and she describes to him the world
as she knows how to describe it,
as she knows how to describe

everything within it;
beautiful
and
unique.

BOOK TWO

IT'S ALWAYS RAINING BOSHO IN MY MIND

FIRST SUMMER

The night is blessed
with a cool breeze, a
pot of hot jasmine tea floating
its sweet aroma between us.

Right now,
we are in a beautiful place.

Basho has a voice like no other.
He is the words of beauty
in a world of violence.

He is the memory of Edo period Japan
washing away
the shogun horrors.

He does not talk
about the Japan fuelled by greed
and corruption.

He does not talk
about the shogun
and the samurai.

He focuses only on
the great beauties of the world,
yet there is a sincere pain
behind his eyes.

He sips his jasmine tea and smiles,
he talks of summer nights
and the joys of nature.

The things which make his heart happy.

Behind all of that
there is genuine sadness.

His smile crinkles
his beautiful face
and a tear rolls down his cheek,
catching in the canvas of his skin.

The words spoken
have the cryptically beautiful resonance
of his poetry.

I fell in love with a creature too beautiful for words.

and everything forever onwards
is washed in Basho poetry and Edo paintings.

PAINTED DRAGONS

We sit on the floor and let
the music of other places drift in
through the open window.

A table between us and a scroll of paper.
The wind, a visitor, rustling paper, ruffling hair,
the night of a winter's storm spent
painting by lamplight.

From the house next door,
a string family playing their chamber music
in puzzling time signatures wrapped in
key signatures which sound like they've been passed
down a chain of delicate musical hands through
the eras only to land
on the doorstep of the house next to us.

Basho strikes a black line on the paper,
a bold mark which can not be removed.

He returns his brush and watches the paper,
waits. Like he's playing some form of solitaire,
searching for the right place, the right moment to
leave his mark.

His lines intersect and he
returns to waiting, listening to strings when
suddenly
a casual hip hop beat drops in on us
and the chamber session becomes
simply reinvented
as the picture between us
begins to take shape.

Here comes the rain,
blending the down-tempo rhythm and the strings
and the painting with patience, mark after
mark, shape after shape,
letting the image take hold.

A tree in bloom with
such orchestral flowers can
only live so long.

In the picture I see a lake's reflection flipped
to his blossoming tree, the careful curves
of Basho's brush, movements like a wand
casting spells.

The tree's limbs twist their way outward
and bend their way to the sky,
surrender to song and to breeze,
open up and reveal their true nature

the limbs of secret dragons.

A beat. An unexpected coming together
of all things. A network of shapes and lines,
of sounds,
and winter gives way to new life,
the season's end
song's end,
strings repeating the sound of silence.

Dragons dancing in the sky in the night time
and no one knows they exist,
such is the fury of their silence,
the beauty of their mythology.

AND THE CITY SLIPS AWAY

Basho is the builder of this world,
the countless creatures hanging on every beat,
the rhythm to his words,
the shapes,
the lines,
the forming of a resonant cluster of thoughts
like a paper boat floating downstream
becoming one with the fish, one
with the river and
drifting off along different paths and
running through the wet fingers of
those creatures of curiosity.

Each path leads to the same place.

Here is a paper boat washed to pieces,
here is the ink leaking and dribbling
and forming little black clouds, the wash
of trees and rivers and dragons swimming
through them invisible

but no less beautiful.

The river runs right through
this house and fish run through the river.
We catch the boat in our fingers but it passes
through us.

We are the ones to see it through and
we are the ones to send it off.

Outside, where the house
next door plays their chamber songs,
is drifting down stream.

Another window shows the river becoming wider,
dislocating us from the houses around us, the
ancient Edo structures, the villages, temples, shrines.

The modern classrooms, the apartment
buildings and skyscrapers,
the cranes—both bird and machine alike—paper floating
down the river, the ink of their image bleeding out.

Cloud-blossoms in the
water. City slips away.
Dragon swims circles.

ATEMPORAL KOI POND

The river takes us away,
the music drifts to silence,
to the sound of crickets, birds, and
frogs.

We're not in Edo any more.
We're not in Tokyo, not in Japan.

The shadowplay theatre out the window
indicates some hybrid of New York, London,
and Berlin. That is not the truth of it either.

Low hanging clouds rolling through
a mountain village. Castle in the sky, in
the clouds floating and rolling along. A rogue
empire of shapes and shadows. The crisp sounds
of a land overrun by nature.

Hollow winds piping their songs into the cool air.

Come, Basho says.
I follow him out into the fog.
The path before us is yellowed like old parchment.
We paint our footprints on it.

Down the path, passing houses occupied by
different versions of Basho. There is a child,
a mother, a monkey, a tiger and a dog.

All of them him.

All of them living in his image,
all of them drowning in the painting of
this place.

Shadowplay reveals the houses,
sprung up right here for us to see.

The different identities, split paths
all leading back to him. All leading down
the parchment path, all towards the atemporal koi pond.

There, Basho is seated on the grass by it.

How one moment we were headed towards it
and the next moment
like a channel changing
he is not the man exploring this place with me
but the one who is the place,
always,
here in the moment,
timeless,
one with nature,

breathless,
opened mind, heart, soul,
wonderful,
flowing out into the pond,
beautiful,
swims with fishes,
atemporal.

Dirt under fingernails,
grass prickling palms.

SHADOWPLAY

Shadows in the pond
gently forming Basho's face.
Fish swims through it, gone.

A TRAIL OF HAIKU

Basho disappears into the pond
becomes it
becomes everything around it.

He leaves a trail of haiku in his wake.

In the pond, four haiku in a circle floating,
one
for each season in the year,
the way nature goes and
Basho follows
or maybe nature follows him.

ENDLESS TSUNAMI

In the world,
in all of the worlds gathered here
brought on by giant waves
and giant transformations made

Basho's words are lost
amongst the waves and waves
of an endless tsunami.

The beauty and terror a sensation
parallel to the image of giving birth.

Worlds washed away and making room
for new worlds.

Basho is the branch of a cherry blossom tree
floating in sea foam. He is a whisper in the wind.
His shadow brushes off the mountains at sunset,
that golden peak of day, an image in an instant gone.

I search for Basho
through a sea of endless tsunami
and his words, his haiku are nestled
so small
in the tiny spaces of this world.

So sublime is the nature of his art.

The parchment of his painted landscape
and hidden dragons
is not hung up on any wall.
It burns on the fire,
fleeting beauty of its lines.
It goes soggy and
comes apart in the water.

You can not hold Basho in his place.
You can not know what he is doing
or where he's gone.

He is gone,
yet this world is full of him.

The world becomes him,
The bluebird calls to him and
sings his name: Basho.

THE BRUSHSTROKE DRAGON

The words are sparse.

They are beautiful and fleeting.

We chase them, but as fast as we chase
them, they evaporate faster,
gone.

Lanterns rising to
a sky bathed in the light of
a new sun dawning.

A sky flooded with these lanterns
burning bright. Chasing a trail of
paper lanterns hidden in the trees.

The poetry is always just beyond my reach
and beyond it still is the
elusive poet, Basho. Beyond himself,
a brushstroke dragon sleeping,

never to be disturbed.

A gift to the world
entirely undeserved
just like the magic of the true haiku
the precious words connected
to form an image so crystalline simple
and yet so delicate and complex.

One misplaced word
and everything becomes unraveled.

*FESTIVAL OF THE PLACE THAT IS
AND IS NOT HERE*

Gone beneath the sunset,
beneath the waves
it is gone.

Through the mist and the mountains,
the myth of the dragon in the real world,
that is all I need.

I am a ghost caught in the breeze,
chasing phantom dragons,
drinking in the sunlight and the stars,
the razor edge of a tail, a claw so sharp,
a wing so leathery tough.

It doesn't matter that I find the dragon.

What matters is the lanterns illuminating space,
revealing wonder, the simple beauty that illuminates
everything we see and renders it a painting or
a poem of Basho's invention.

There is the dragon.
There is its shadow.
There is the charcoal scent of its scorched breath.
A heavy sigh, a hard truth to swallow.
There is no dragon.

We pursue always what we can not have,
whether it is real or projected, imagined.
Whether or not it is true.

Only the festival is true.
Only those within it,
those who listen to its song,
light a lantern,
let it go.

The dragon just beyond our fingertips
sitting just beyond our eternal reach,
that is Basho.

The old man paddling hard, going nowhere
paddling upstream into the river,
that is Basho.

Playing words and playing music,
playing everything the world pulling itself apart
dissecting its wounds and wisdom,
admiring the beauty of its scars,
that is also him.

BASHO MULTIPLIED ONE THOUSAND TIMES

A samurai sitting on a rock,
death by assassination,
death by combat,
death by honourable suicide.

Family and history and home,
blood smeared on the path,
splatter flicked from the edge
of a samurai sword.

Beauty and horror,
nobility and chaos,
shogun and ronin.

Not a haiku.
Not a haiku for the words,
the images.

There is in this world a million horrors,
with only one thousand Basho to balance out.

What blood drips from blade,
what severed heads and poison darts,
what bombs exploded and planes
fallen from the sky.

A history of death and disaster,
and in that history a memory,
an image.

Pick your words, Basho,
make the world beautiful again.

NUJABES SYMPHONY IN THE SKY

Basho disintegrating
Basho dissolving into everything
clouds forming Basho
forming haiku in the sky.

He is everywhere you can't escape from.

Paintings in the sky
and dragons
floating blissfully
and the cloud chamber music family.
The wind, the sky sings
rain clouds beautifully percussive.

Nujabes in the sky dropping songs
like rain, music to the earth,
soil drinks it up, turns it into
the grass that grows in unlikely places,
the trees that sing a call and response,
an extension of the song

the samurai dance
samurai champloo,
Basho reincarnated as hip hop artist
in the sky.

The space between two worlds
light as a feather
the aruarian dance
a beautiful thing
water forming a pool in cupped hands
drink it in
the sound
the electric landscape
the symphony of sampling
taken to a beautiful place.

Drink it in.

*DRAGON RAIN AND NIGHT-TIME
WISDOM*

In the fields, in the symphonic plains
and mountaintops,
in the first days of a city,
in the days and months and years
of a city being born
in the nation that you know so well
there is the nestled spirit of your mind,
an egg.

A dragon formed with ink and music,
a dragon of words connected and fearsome,
indestructible.

The moment of a city dying,
a landscape forever altered or
a spiritual shift, a cultural death.

A funeral on
a rainy day, flowers dance
for the young tombstones.

He knows all of this
and leaves me chasing ghosts
and poems, it's like I don't know him
at all, only his words a warped truth.

Time and day and year and place,
objects and living creatures,
movements,
all stripped down
to this simple logic
captured so swiftly in the moment
a master of the form.

Night and day as revolutions
on the same place,
chasing moments
and writing them down,
the world constructed not as it is,
but as he exists within it,
chasing dragons,
the beauty of the horizon
and what is just beyond it,
the beauty of the surreal
the sublime,
the imagined.

Life is a beautiful thing.
Death is a beautiful thing.

The world has turned
and left me here,
chasing Basho chasing
dragons through real and unreal worlds,

following the dreams and words
of a man who exists
only in bones and words and memories,
who used to be a formless, thoughtless
thing not yet born.

He is madness reincarnate
as the dragon is born of madness
and kindly he shows me what I know,
he is always already real and alive
and ready to walk
the mountain path of his legacy.

As the rain forms a bridge
with the night time,
that is when the dragons come out,
that is what he teaches me.

Hands rush through the koi pond
become fish themselves
and the hands themselves become lost.

Beauty becomes dragons.

All the magnificent, noble things in the world.

Here is a house, a garden, a river.

The home of zen, that
shared place of peace and chaos,
dream of life and death.

DRAGON SONG

I fell in love with a creature too beautiful for words.

Painting of a dragon in the sky.

The beauty of that which does not exist.

The simple beauty of Basho poetry.

The love and tenderness.

Heartwarming Basho, heartbroken poet,
cultural enigma,
a legacy of words engraved
and fingers pointed
in the direction of them
and the declaration
this is him
this is the guy you heard about
the words you read
or better yet

this is what he has become
this is what he left us.

A love unreal,
the swoon of a dragon song,
that which has already gone
and always will linger,
the history of poetry and music,
nature and art,
tea ceremonies,
scenes held precious, vivid, dynamic in the mind
unforgotten.

*LOVE FOR THE THING THAT IS
NOT REAL*

The dragon is indestructible.
It is so close I can feel its breath.

Can you feel it?

It swims metallic, scales glistening in the
river flow. Wet fingers, wet toes.

Can you feel it?

Whiskers of a mythic sea monster.
Like a ghost passing through you.

Can you feel it?

The self-sustaining myth eating itself extinct.
Eating itself immortal, the ouroboros.
A tattoo on your heel.
Fireworks in the sky.

To believe in something once it's gone,
even if it may not have been there ever,
even if not at all, to still believe.

Do you feel it?

POEM FLOWING RIVER REAL

Here is the river
washed everything away.

All the houses, cities, dreams.

Here is the river flowing
through mountains and memories,
through galaxies.

In the river
there is a poem,
in the river a paper boat,
a painting, a dragon swimming
with fishes.

Light hits the water,
the sleek and shiny things
beneath its current,
golden.

*PAINTING OF THAT BASHO
FEELING*

What more could you want
than to be in the same room as him
and be reminded that the outside world embraces you.

In the outside world there is the feeling of home.

A blanket of leaves,
a breeze,
a family of animals
or simply just the chaos of the nature
of such creatures in the wild
or such wild creatures in the city.

Car slams breaks,
lights shined on scared beasts
learning that the world goes from
forest to metropolis in a number of
footsteps.

Seasons change,

the city stays the same.

It looks like all the others,
it makes all the same promises.

Live within it,
there is no living without it.

Here in the house,
sliding doors and steaming cups
of jasmine tea,
tapestries on walls overlapping,
paintings of Edo culture,
paintings of the truly beautiful women
and samurai and dragons of the day,
ships and merchants,
temples and poems.

A ghostly world that is both his
and not.

You know when you read it,
when you look upon a painting
and you get that Basho feeling,

he is the thread which connects us together.

THE ILLUSTRATED WORLD OF
HAIKU

A woman sits in the corner of this room
walls becoming smaller
and she plucks the strings of her instrument,
something with a name lying just beyond my tongue,
something which haunts.

Close your eyes and inhale.
The intoxicating memories of a place you've never been.
A man you've never met.
A love you can't imagine.

Heartbroken by an illusion broken,
sitting, smouldering, smoking,
words curling in the air.

As he paints with patience
and reveals rivers and forests both
real and imagined,
as he recites love songs
for the fierce, beautiful, and thoroughly

fictional dragon which plagues his thoughts
his dreams

his words are pictures,
short phrases clustered around
the shapes of silence.

FOUND DRAGON FRIEND

It's raining
and the world around me is turning
into a mess of words
a flowing river of haiku imagery
the simplicity of a current
which direction can not be moved.

I am the dragon flowing through it
while the master of words
is lost in a world which
has no room left
for such mysticism and beauty.

A dying art, a tradition fading,
and as his words, his vision is always here,
he is not.

The love of dragons, capturing that
rare beast, finding that familiar thing
which makes your life's goal

dedicated to a fiction,
a reality washed over by what people see,
a goal through the rain,
worthwhile,
through the summer heat,
through the seasons of nature
dying off and being born again,
a sustained belief in something
which may or may not survive,
which may not be there for you
tomorrow,
a friend right now, a haiku, here.

LOST DRAGON, BASHO FOUND

A burial, in the rain,
a hole full of water.

This is not the city or the mountain,
the forest or the house.

Find him they said,
the dragons.
Bring him home.

He is eternal.
I sit and watch him paint forever
his haiku rendering immortal
the world through his eyes.

Dragon fades away,
bury it.
Basho comes home,
writes into his life
changed the world

the people of the years
and generations such generations beyond him
fully clothed in different worlds,
dragons apart,
he is still here, meaning something different,
yet still exactly the same.

Bury him.

I will know no other.
Dreamscapes are built on this.

BASHO RAIN

Clouds come together
smiling, it's always raining
Basho in my mind.

ACKNOWLEDGMENTS

I owe a huge thank you to Christoph and Leza for publishing this book. These poems have gone through so many stages of submission and acceptance and collapse and resubmission and plans which never quite eventuated due to poor timing or other unfortunate circumstances. It feels amazing not only that this book is even happening at all, but also that CLASH Books have really helped to make it the best version that it could possibly be.

I also owe a huge debt of gratitude to the Perth poetry scene, and in particular to Spoken Word Perth, as it was at this small event back when it was held in the echoing halls of Fremantle Prison where I first performed poems from this book. Also to Luke Farrell for allowing me to perform an excerpt at his band's (Slaughterhouse Five) single launch.

ABOUT THE AUTHOR

S.T. Cartledge writes weird fiction and poetry. His work includes the Orphanarium and Cherry Blossom Eyes from Eraserhead Press and his debut poetry collection, Beautiful Madness. He lives in Perth, Western Australia along with his partner and child, two dogs, and six cats.

ALSO BY CLASH BOOKS

TRAGEDY QUEENS: STORIES INSPIRED BY LANA DEL REY & SYLVIA PLATH
Edited by Leza Cantoral

GIRL LIKE A BOMB
Autumn Christian

CENOTE CITY
Monique Quintana

99 POEMS TO CURE WHATEVER'S WRONG WITH YOU OR CREATE THE PROBLEMS YOU NEED
Sam Pink

THIS BOOK IS BROUGHT TO YOU BY MY STUDENT LOANS
Megan J. Kaleita

PAPI DOESN'T LOVE ME NO MORE
Anna Suarez

ARSENAL/SIN DOCUMENTOS
Francesco Levato

THIS IS A HORROR BOOK

Charles Austin Muir

I'M FROM NOWHERE

Lindsay Lerman

HEAVEN IS A PHOTOGRAPH

Christine Sloan Stoddard

FOGHORN LEGHORN

Big Bruiser Dope Boy

TRY NOT TO THINK BAD THOUGHTS

Art by Matthew Revert

SEQUELLAND

Jay Clayton-Joslin

JAH HILLS

Unathi Slasha

GIMME THE LOOT: STORIES INSPIRED BY NOTORIOUS B.I.G

Edited by Gabino Iglesias

THE MISADVENTURES OF A GILTED JOURNALIST

Justin Little

NEW VERONIA

M.S. Coe

SPORTS CENTER POEMS

Poetry by Christoph Paul & Art by Jim Agpalza

THE HAUNTING OF THE PARANORMAL ROMANCE AWARDS

Christoph Paul & Mandy De Sandra

GODLESS HEATHENS: CONVERSATIONS WITH ATHEISTS

Edited by Andrew J. Rausch

DARK MOONS RISING IN A STARLESS NIGHT

Mame Bougouma Diene

GODDAMN KILLING MACHINES

David Agranoff

NOHO GLOAMING & THE CURIOUS CODA OF ANTHONY SANTOS

Daniel Knauf (Creator of HBO's Carnivàle)

IF YOU DIED TOMORROW I WOULD EAT YOUR CORPSE

Wrath James White

THE ANARCHIST KOSHER COOKBOOK

Maxwell Bauman

HORROR FILM POEMS

Poetry by Christoph Paul & Art by Joel Amat Güell

NIGHTMARES IN ECSTASY

Brendan Vidito

THE VERY INEFFECTIVE HAUNTED HOUSE

Jeff Burk

ZOMBIE PUNKS FUCK OFF

Edited by Sam Richard

THIS BOOK AIN'T NUTTIN TO FUCK WITH: A WU-TANG TRIBUTE ANTHOLOGY

Edited by Christoph Paul

WALK HAND IN HAND INTO EXTINCTION - STORIES INSPIRED BY TRUE DETECTIVE

Edited by Christoph Paul & Leza Cantoral

WE PUT THE LIT IN LITERARY

CL◀SH

CLASHBOOKS.COM

www.ingramcontent.com/pod-product-compliance
Lightning Source LLC
Chambersburg PA
CBHW020125130526
44591CB00032B/527